TensorFlow Developer Certificate Exam Practice Tests 2024 Made Easy

Mr Troy

Published by Mr Troy, 2024.

While every precaution has been taken in the preparation of this book, the publisher assumes no responsibility for errors or omissions, or for damages resulting from the use of the information contained herein.

TENSORFLOW DEVELOPER CERTIFICATE EXAM PRACTICE TESTS 2024 MADE EASY

First edition. February 3, 2024.

ISBN: 979-8224603350

Written by Mr Troy.

Mr. Troy

TensorFlow Developer Certificate Exam
Practice Tests
2024 made easy

1 Getting started

1.1 Intro

In addition to this book, we offer a video-based on- line course available on Udemy. It can be accessed through the following link: TensorFlow Developer[1] Certificate Exam Practice Tests[2].

Hello and welcome to 'TensorFlow Developer Cer- tificate Exam Practice Tests 2024 made easy'! I'm Mr Troy, your guide on this exciting journey towards passing the certification exam and getting your certificate.

The TensorFlow Developer Certificate is a game- changer. It's not just a certification; it's your ticket

---

1. https://www.udemy.com/course/tensorflow-developer-certificate-exam-practice-tests/?referralCode=5BDEEC5D3C9D0BA109F8

2. https://www.udemy.com/course/tensorflow-developer-certificate-exam-practice-tests/?referralCode=5BDEEC5D3C9D0BA109F8

to a world of opportunities in Machine Learning and AI.

By completing this course and passing the exam, you'll be eligible for inclusion in the TensorFlow Cer- tificate Network, a prime spot where recruiters find top TensorFlow talent.

Plus, you can showcase your success by adding a Digital Certificate and Badge to your LinkedIn pro- files.

This course is specially designed for fast and ef- fective learning, taking less than 2 hours to com- plete. With our concise yet comprehensive approach, you can get ready and pass the exam in under two hours. Perfect for those with a tight schedule!

Whether you prefer Google Colab. . . , Jupyter Notebooks. . . , or PyCharm. . . , our practice tests can be run in any of these environments.

We offer a diverse range of practice tests, includ- ing key areas like Linear Regression, Image Clas- sification, Natural Language Processing, and Time Series and Sequences. This ensures a well-rounded preparation for every aspect of the TensorFlow De- veloper Certificate Exam.

Our detailed TensorFlow solution code and step- by-step practical guidance are designed to enhance your problem-solving skills, ensuring you're ready for the exam and beyond.

Ready to take the next step in your AI and Ma- chine Learning career? Enroll in 'TensorFlow De- veloper Certificate Exam Practice Tests 2024 made easy' today, and embark on a journey of practical exercises and guaranteed success!

1.2 All resources

Links to all the resources used in this course can be found on the last page of this book due to secu- rity concerns and keeping the resources from being abused.

- All the practice tests and solutions in Python format (*.py). They have the same format as the real exams and should be run using Pycharm IDE. We will go through them one by one later: See the last page

- All the practice tests and solutions in note- book format (*.ipynb). If you are familiar with Jupyter/Google Colab/Kaggle notebooks. They are ready for you to run: See the last page

- Python ebook

- TensorFlow certificate homepage: https://www.tensorflow.org/certificate
- Candidate handbook:
- https://www.tensorflow.org/static/extras/cert[3]
- Handbook for setting up your computer for the exam: https://www.tensorflow.org/extras/cert/Settin[4]
- Trueability's handbook (Trueability is affiliated with Google's TensorFlow to conduct the exam)
  - _____ •   https://utility.trueability.com/google/tensor-[5] flow/ Instructions for taking the TensorFlow Ce[6]
- My certificate for your reference: https://www.credential.net/f7b087a1-a977-[7] 4b84-bdd6-fb7d92eae41b[8]
- Certificate network:
https://developers.google.com/certification/di[9]

---

3.   https://www.tensorflow.org/static/extras/cert/TF_Certificate_Candidate_Handbook.pdf

4.   https://www.tensorflow.org/extras/cert/Setting_Up_TF_Developer_Certificate_Exam.pdf

5.   https://utility.trueability.com/google/tensor-flow/

Instructions_for_taking_the_TensorFlow_Certificate_exam.pdf

6.   https://utility.trueability.com/google/tensor-flow/

Instructions_for_taking_the_TensorFlow_Certificate_exam.pdf

7.   https://www.credential.net/f7b087a1-a977-4b84-bdd6-fb7d92eae41b

8.   https://www.credential.net/f7b087a1-a977-4b84-bdd6-fb7d92eae41b

9.   https://developers.google.com/certification/directory/tensorflow

1.3 Questions and concerns

If you have any questions or comments about this course's content or delivery, please do not hesitate to contact me either via email at troyphattran@gmail.com, or via Linkedin https://www.linkedin.com/in/trientran/, and I'll get back to you ASAP (usually within 24 hours).

2 Prepare your exam environ- ment

2.1 Notes

This chapter covers the setup of Python and Py- Charm, necessary for the TensorFlow exam.

If you're comfortable with Google Colab, Kag- gle Notebooks, or Jupyter Notebooks. . . , you can use them for the practice tests. Just simply copy the code from our practice tests (*.py files) to your favourite notebook environment. Install Python and PyCharm later when you are ready for the exam.

If you're new to Colab and Jupyter, follow the in- stallation steps for Python and PyCharm provided here.

2.2 Install Python

In this section, I'll guide you through the process of installing Python 3.9, the required version for Ten- sorFlow, on your computer. If you're using a Mac, it may already have Python installed, but we need to ensure it's the correct version for TensorFlow. For Windows users, you'll need to install Python 3.9.

Let's begin by visiting

https://www[10].tensorflo[11]w.org/certificate[12] and open- ing the Candidate Handbook. This PDF handbook outlines the exam procedure and provides a link to set up your computer for the exam.

In the handbook, click on "Exam environment" and then follow the link to "Set up your environment to take the TensorFlow Developer Certificate Exam" PDF for detailed technical requirements.

Now, let's focus on the required Python ver- sion. Google's TensorFlow team recommends Python 3.9, specifically version 3.9.2. To get it, go to www.python.org/downloads[13] and search for Python

3.9.2. Click "Download" and scroll down. If you're on macOS, choose the "macOS 64-bit installer" option. For Windows users, select either "32 bit" or "64 bit" depending on your computer's hardware.

Mac users, be aware that there are two macOS options: one for Intel processors and one for Univer- sal/Apple chipset. Since my Macbook has an Intel processor, I'll download the macOS 64-bit Intel in- staller.

After downloading the installer, open it and follow the installation process.

For macOS users, there's an additional step. Af- ter installing Python, you'll need to add SSL cer- tificates for internet connectivity. To do this, open

10.   http://www.tensorflow.org/certificate

11.   http://www.tensorflow.org/certificate

12.   http://www.tensorflow.org/certificate

13.   http://www.python.org/downloads

Finder, go to the Applications folder, locate the Python 3.9 folder, and double-click on "Install Cer- tificates.command" to install the necessary certifi- cates.

That's it! You're now ready to use Python 3.9 with TensorFlow. Thanks for reading.

2.3 Tip for Mac user

_For Mac users, if you receive an URLError related to SSL certificate verification (url- lib.error.URLError: ¡urlopenerror [SSL: CERTIFI- CATE VERIFY FAILED]), install an SSL certificate by navigating to Finder ¿ Applications ¿ Python3.8 folder (or your Python version) and running the "Install Certificates.command" file.

2.4 Install Pycharm

Pycharm has both Professional (paid) and Commu- nity (free) versions. In this course, I use **PyCharm 2023.2.3 Community Edition** to run all our prac- tice tests.

_Note: even though the handbook https://www.tensorflow.org/ extras/cert/Setting Up[14] suggests installing the latest version of Pycharm

---

14. https://www.tensorflow.org/extras/cert/Setting_Up_TF_Developer_Certificate_Exam.pdf

(https://www.jetbrains.com/pycharm/download/), there could be **compatibility issues** with the **TensorFlow Certificate Exam plugin**. Therefore, I highly recommend using the specific version of PyCharm that is utilised in this course. Direct links (Note that the direct links to this version are subject to change by JetBrains at any time):

Mac users: https://download-[15] cdn.jetbrains.com/python/ pycharm-community-[16] 2023.2.3.dmg[17] (intel CPU)

https://download.jetbrains.com/python/pychar[18] community-2023.2.3-aarch64.dmg[19] (apple silicon CPU)

Window users: https://download-[20] cdn.jetbrains.com/python/ pycharm-community-[21] 2023.2.3.exe[22] (32 bit)

https://download.jetbrains.com/python/pychar[23] community-2023.2.3-aarch64.exe[24] (64 bit)

Linux: https://download.jetbrains.com/python/pychar[25] community-2023.2.3.tar.gz[26]   (32   bit) https://download.jetbrains.com/python/pychar[27] community-2023.2.3-aarch64.tar.gz[28] (64 bit)

---

15.   https://download-cdn.jetbrains.com/python/pycharm-community-2023.2.3.dmg

16.   https://download-cdn.jetbrains.com/python/pycharm-community-2023.2.3.dmg

17.   https://download-cdn.jetbrains.com/python/pycharm-community-2023.2.3.dmg

18.   https://download.jetbrains.com/python/pycharm-community-2023.2.3-aarch64.dmg

19.   https://download.jetbrains.com/python/pycharm-community-2023.2.3-aarch64.dmg

20.   https://download-cdn.jetbrains.com/python/pycharm-community-2023.2.3.exe

21.   https://download-cdn.jetbrains.com/python/pycharm-community-2023.2.3.exe

22.   https://download-cdn.jetbrains.com/python/pycharm-community-2023.2.3.exe

23.   https://download.jetbrains.com/python/pycharm-community-2023.2.3-aarch64.exe

24.   https://download.jetbrains.com/python/pycharm-community-2023.2.3-aarch64.exe

25.   https://download.jetbrains.com/python/pycharm-community-2023.2.3.tar.gz

26.   https://download.jetbrains.com/python/pycharm-community-2023.2.3.tar.gz

27.   https://download.jetbrains.com/python/pycharm-community-2023.2.3-aarch64.tar.gz

28.   https://download.jetbrains.com/python/pycharm-community-2023.2.3-aarch64.tar.gz

Older versions of Pycharm can be found at https://www.jetbrains.com/edu-[29] products/download/ other-PCE.html[30]

---

29. https://www.jetbrains.com/edu-products/download/other-PCE.html

30. https://www.jetbrains.com/edu-products/download/other-PCE.html

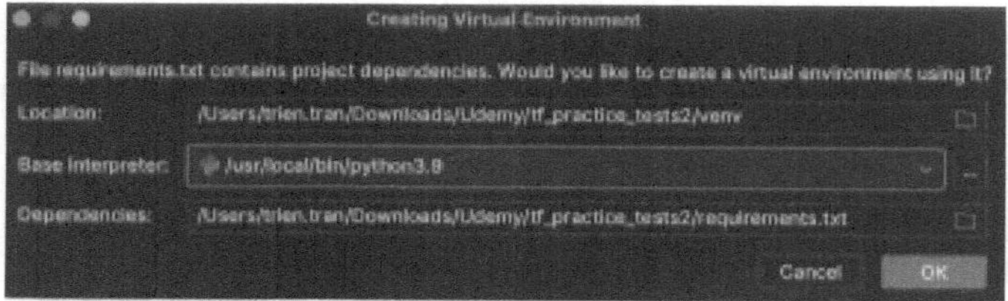

Figure 1: Enter Caption

2.5 Python packages & exam plugin

In the previous step, you downloaded our Tensor- Flow project to your computer. In this video, I will guide you on how to install the Python packages re- quired for training our deep learning models and the TensorFlow Certificate Plugin, a crucial infrastruc- ture component for you to take the exam.

First things first, please open PyCharm. Then, click 'Open' or go to 'File ¿ Open' and navigate to the folder where you downloaded our TensorFlow project. If a dialog pops up asking if you trust and want to open the project? Please click 'Trust Project'.

Upon your first launch, Pycharm is asking you to create a virtual environment. A virtual environ- ment in this Pycharm project is where we host all

*of the required Python libraries and specify the base Python interpreter.
"File requirements.txt..." What it means is, in Pycharm projects,
requirements.txt is like a Python library listing file. It lists all of the Python
li- braries you want to inject into your Python projects. Here, dependencies
just simply mean Python li- braries or Python packages.*

*Now, we want to ensure Python 3.9 has been se- lected because it is the
required Python version that we discussed in a previous video.*

*So, after you click OK, Pycharm will automatically download all the
Python packages specified in re- quirements.txt. It's going to take a bit of
time to finish that.*

Notice that PyCharm's User Interface has a new look. If you are
used to the previous classic UI, please click this settings icon and select
'Switch to Classic UI. . . '.

At the bottom of the left pane, you can find require- ments.txt.

____If you double-click on this file to open it, you can see all the
required Python library packages I have prepared for you as advised in
the Set- ting Up TF Developer Certificate Exam handbook.

As you can see here on page numbered 10 of the handbook, we need
all these installed:

numpy==1.24.3 pandas==2.0.3 Pillow==10.0.0 scipy==1.10.1 tensorflow==2.13.0 tensorflow- datasets==4.9.2

If the handbook suggests newer versions, feel free to update them here in this requirements.txt file ac- cordingly. (stop recording and wait until the instal- lation is finished)

So, after Pycharm has finished installing pack- ages, you can double-check if these packages are in- stalled by clicking the 'Python Packages' icon at the bottom left corner. Type in the search bar the name of a Python package such as Numpy and press en- ter. Then you should see the Numpy package listed under the 'Installed' list like this. If not, then you can just install it manually from here by selecting the package, choosing a version, and hitting 'Install Package'.

Next, The file Readme.md is where you can find all the tips I share with you in this course. I added them all here to make it easier for you to take some notes before taking the real exam.

As you can see, the left pane also displays the entire project structure containing all the practice tests used in this course such as image classifica- tion, linear regression, natural language processing, and time series and sequences. In each of these categories, I have prepared both questions and solu- tions for you. To run a Python solution program, you can either right-click on the file and select 'Run', or use this combined keyboard shortcut; or double click on the file to open it, then select the current file and click this 'Run' icon.

Our last step is installing the TensorFlow Exam Plugin. Let's open the settings window. On Microsoft Windows and Linux computers, select 'File' and then 'Settings'. In MacOS, click 'PyCharm/Settings' in recent MacOS or 'Preferences' in older MacOS; and Then in the settings screen, go to 'Plugins', select 'MarketPlace', and search for. . . 'TensorFlow Developer Certificate'. Click the green 'Install' but- ton. . . accept. . . . and then restart the IDE when prompted.

After Pycharm has been relaunched, you should be able to see the orange Start Exam button up here. But believe me, you are not going to take the exam now unless you have purchased the exam and are ready for it.

That's it. I just walked you through the initial setup for PyCharm and our TensorFlow practice exam. Good luck, and I'll see you in the next chapter.

3 Linear Regression

3.1 Question

```
# Copyright (c) 2023, Troy Phat Tran (Mr.
    ↪ Troy).
    # Linear Regression Question - Integer
    # You have been given two arrays: x_array and
    ↪ y_array, each containing a number of
    ↪ integer values.
    # The x_array contains input values and y_array
    ↪ contains corresponding output values. Using
    ↪ TensorFlow,
    # create a neural network model that can
    ↪ predict the output of a given input value x
    ↪ based on the relationship
    # between x and y.
    # Your task is to fill in the missing parts of
    ↪ the regression_model function (where
    ↪ commented as "ADD CODE HERE").
import numpy as np
```

```python
from keras import Sequential
from keras.saving import load_model


def regression_model():
    # Define the input and output data
    ↪ (corresponding to "y = 10x + 5")
    x_array = np.array([-1, 0, 1, 2, 3, 4, 5,
    ↪ 6], dtype=int)
    y_array = np.array([-5, 5, 15, 25, 35, 45,
    ↪ 55, 65], dtype=int)
    # Define the model architecture
    model = Sequential([

      # ADD CODE HERE

    ])
    # Compile the model # ADD CODE HERE
    # Train the model # ADD CODE HERE
    return model
```

```python
# ================DO NOT EDIT THIS
↪ PART=================================
if name == ' main ':
    # Run and save your model
    my_model      =      regression_model()      filepath      =
"regression_model_1.h5" my_model.save(filepath)
    # Reload the saved model
    saved_model = load_model(filepath)
    # Show the model architecture
    saved_model.summary()
    # Test the model on some new data
    x_test = np.array([7, 8, 9, 10])
    y_test   =   np.array([75,   85,   95,   105])   predictions   =
saved_model.predict(x_test)
    # Print the predictions and expected values
    for i in range(len(x_test)):

        print("x = {:.0f}, expected y = {:.0f},
        ↪ predicted y =
        ↪ {:.0f}".format(x_test[i],
        ↪ y_test[i], predictions[i][0]))
```

```
# Evaluate the model on the test data
test_loss = saved_model.evaluate(x_test,
↪ y_test)
print("Test loss:
↪ {:.2f}".format(test_loss))
```

3.2 Solution

```
# Copyright (c) 2023, Troy Phat Tran (Mr.
    ↪ Troy).
    import numpy as np
    from keras import Sequential from keras.layers import Dense
    from keras.saving import load_model


def regression_model():
    # Define the input and output data
↪ (corresponding to "y =    10x + 5")
x_array = np.array([-1, 0, 1, 2, 3, 4,   5,
↪ 6], dtype=int)
y_array = np.array([-5, 5, 15, 25, 35, 45,
↪ 55, 65], dtype=int)
```

```python
# Define the model architecture
model = Sequential([

  # ADD CODE HERE
  Dense(units=1, input_shape=[1])

])
# Compile the model # ADD CODE HERE
model.compile(optimizer='sgd',
↪ loss='mean_squared_error')
# Train the model # ADD CODE HERE
model.fit(x=x_array, y=y_array,
↪ epochs=1000)
return model
```

4 Image classification

4.1 Question 1 - grayscale image

Copyright (c) 2023, Troy Phat Tran (Mr.
↪ Troy).
Yann LeCun and Corinna Cortes hold the
↪ copyright of MNIST dataset, which is a
↪ derivative work from original NIST
datasets. MNIST dataset is made available
↪ under the terms of the Creative Commons
↪ Attribution-Share Alike 3.0 license.
Question:
Create a classifier for the MNIST dataset
↪ which includes black-and-white images of 10
↪ digits (0-9). Link:

#

↪ https://www.tensorflow.org/datasets/catalog/[31]
The input shape should be (28, 28, 1) because
↪ each image has 28*28 pixels and is
↪ grayscale.

---

31. http://www.tensorflow.org/datasets/catalog/

```
# Your task is to fill in the missing parts of
<-> the code block (where commented as "ADD
<-> CODE HERE").
from keras import Sequential from keras.datasets import mnist
from keras.saving import load_model
```

```
# Use Keras dataset
    def my_model():
    # Load the MNIST dataset
    dataset = mnist
    (x_train, y_train), (x_test, y_test) =
<-> dataset.load_data()
    # Normalize the input data
    x_train    =    x_train.astype('float32')    /    255.0    x_test    =
x_test.astype('float32') / 255.0
    # Define the model architecture
    model = Sequential([

      # ADD CODE HERE

    ])
    # Compile the model
```

```python
# ADD CODE HERE
# Define the early stopping callback # ADD CODE HERE
# Train the model with the early stopping
↪ callback
# ADD CODE HERE
return model




# ================DO NOT EDIT THIS
↪ PART===================================
if name == ' main ':
# Run and save your model
my_model = my_model()
filepath = "grayscale_model_1.h5" my_model.save(filepath)
# Reload the saved model
saved_model = load_model(filepath)
# Show the model architecture
saved_model.summary()
```

4.2 Solution for Question 1

```
from keras import Sequential
    from keras.callbacks import EarlyStopping from keras.datasets
import mnist
    from keras.layers import Conv2D, MaxPooling2D,
    ↪ Flatten, Dense
    from keras.saving import load_model


def my_model():
    # Load the MNIST dataset
    dataset = mnist
    (x_train, y_train), (x_valid, y_valid) =
    ↪ dataset.load_data()
    # Normalize the input data
    x_train = x_train.astype('float32') / 255.0 x_valid =
x_valid.astype('float32') / 255.0
    # Define the model architecture
    model = Sequential([
```

```
# ADD CODE HERE
Conv2D(filters=32, kernel_size=(3, 3),
↪ activation='relu', input_shape=(28,
↪ 28, 1)),
# black-white images have only one
↪ color channel
MaxPooling2D(pool_size=(2, 2)),
Conv2D(filters=64, kernel_size=(3, 3),
↪ activation='relu'),
MaxPooling2D(pool_size=(2, 2)), Flatten(),
Dense(units=64,      activation='relu'),      Dense(units=10,
activation='softmax')
↪ # units=10 because there are 10
↪ classes/digits in the dataset

])
# Compile the model # ADD CODE HERE
model.compile(optimizer='adam',
↪ loss='sparse_categorical_crossentropy',
↪ metrics=['accuracy'])
# Define the early stopping callback # ADD CODE HERE
```

```
early_stop =
↪ EarlyStopping(monitor='val_accuracy',
↪ patience=5, min_delta=0.01, verbose=1)
# Train the model with the early stopping
↪ callback
# Reshape the data to add the channel
↪ dimension
# ADD CODE HERE
x_train = x_train.reshape((-1, 28, 28, 1))
x_valid = x_valid.reshape((-1, 28, 28, 1)) model.fit(

  x=x_train, y=y_train, epochs=10,
  validation_data=(x_valid, y_valid), callbacks=[early_stop]

)
return model
```

4.3 Question 2 - colour image

```
# Copyright (c) 2023, Troy Phat Tran (Mr.
 ↪ Troy).
# Binary (2-classes) image classification
 ↪ dataset: apple-banana.
# Direct link: #
 ↪ http://dl.dropboxusercontent.com/scl/fi/mw43
# (~7.6 Megabytes)
# Backup direct link:
 ↪ https://trientran.github.io/tf-practice-exam
# This dataset comprises 2 classes namely Apple
 ↪ and Banana, and it has been split into
 ↪ training and validation sets.
# Create a classifier for the given dataset.
 ↪ The required input shape must be 100x100x3
 ↪ (RGB images).
# Your task is to fill in the missing parts of
 ↪ the code block (where commented as "ADD
 ↪ CODE HERE").
import os
```

```python
import zipfile
from urllib.request import urlretrieve
from keras import Sequential
from keras.models import load_model from keras.utils import
↪ image_dataset_from_directory
from tensorflow import cast, float32
from tensorflow.python.data import AUTOTUNE


# A function to rescale/normalize images
def rescale(image, label):
    image = cast(image, float32) / 255.0 return image, label


def binary_model():
    # Define a data folder to extract our
    ↪ compressed dataset to
    data_folder = 'apple-banana/'
    # Download and extract the dataset if not
    ↪ existing
    if not os.path.exists(data_folder):
```

```python
dataset_url =
↪ 'http://dl.dropboxusercontent.com/sc[32]
local_zip = 'apple-banana.zip' urlretrieve(url=dataset_url,
↪ filename=local_zip)
zip_ref =
↪ zipfile.ZipFile(file=local_zip,
↪ mode='r')
zip_ref.extractall(data_folder) zip_ref.close()

# Define image size and batch size
img_size = (0, 0) # ADD CODE HERE: just
↪ update the image size here to match the
↪ requirement
batch_size = 32
# Create the training dataset
# The dataset is already split into
↪ training and validation sets

train_ds          =          image_dataset_from_directory(
directory="apple-banana/train/", seed=1,

image_size=img_size, batch_size=batch_size

)
```

---

32. http://dl.dropboxusercontent.com/sc

```
# Create the validation dataset

  val_ds              =                image_dataset_from_directory(
  directory="apple-banana/validation/", seed=1,

  image_size=img_size, batch_size=batch_size

)
# Rescale images (option 1)
train_ds = train_ds.map(rescale,
↪ num_parallel_calls=AUTOTUNE)
val_ds = val_ds.map(rescale,
↪ num_parallel_calls=AUTOTUNE)
# Configure the dataset for performance #
↪ https://www.tensorflow.org/tutorials/ima³³
train_ds =
↪ train_ds.cache().shuffle(1000).prefetch(
val_ds =
↪ val_ds.cache().prefetch(buffer_size=AUTO
# Define the model architecture
model = Sequential([
```

---

33.   http://www.tensorflow.org/tutorials/ima

```
    # Rescaling(1. / 255,
    ↪ input_shape=(img_size[0],
    ↪ img_size[1], 3)), # Rescale images
    ↪ (option 2)
    # ADD CODE HERE

])
# Compile the model # ADD CODE HERE
# Define the early stopping callback for
↪ val_accuracy
# ADD CODE HERE
# Show the model architecture (optional)
summarize_model(model)
# Train the model with early stopping
↪ callback
# ADD CODE HERE
return model


# ===============DO NOT EDIT THIS
    ↪ PART===================================
```

```
def summarize_model(model): model.summary()
    input_shape = model.layers[0].input_shape print(f'Input shape:
{input_shape}')
```

```
if name == ' main ':
    # Run and save your model my_model = binary_model() filepath =
"binary_rgb_model.h5" my_model.save(filepath)
    # Reload the saved model saved_model = load_model(filepath)
summarize_model(saved_model)
```

4.4 Solution for Question 2

```
import os import zipfile
    from urllib.request import urlretrieve
    from keras import Sequential
    from keras.callbacks import EarlyStopping
```

```
from keras.layers import Conv2D, MaxPooling2D,
↪ Flatten, Dense
from keras.models import load_model from keras.utils import
↪ image_dataset_from_directory
from tensorflow import cast, float32
from tensorflow.python.data import AUTOTUNE


# A function to rescale/normalize images
    def rescale(image, label):
    image = cast(image, float32) / 255.0 return image, label


def binary_model():
    # Define a data folder to extract our
    ↪ compressed dataset to
    data_folder = 'apple-banana/'
    # Download and extract the dataset if not
    ↪ existing

    if not os.path.exists(data_folder): dataset_url =
    ↪ 'http://dl.dropboxusercontent.com/sc³⁴
    local_zip = 'apple-banana.zip'
```

---

34. http://dl.dropboxusercontent.com/sc

```
urlretrieve(url=dataset_url,
↳ filename=local_zip)
zip_ref =
↳ zipfile.ZipFile(file=local_zip,
↳ mode='r')
zip_ref.extractall(data_folder) zip_ref.close()

# Define image size and batch size
img_size = (100, 100)
batch_size = 32
# Create the training dataset
# The dataset is already split into
↳ training and validation sets

train_ds            =            image_dataset_from_directory(
directory="apple-banana/train/", seed=1,

image_size=img_size, batch_size=batch_size

)
# Create the validation dataset

val_ds            =            image_dataset_from_directory(
directory="apple-banana/validation/", seed=1,
```

```
  image_size=img_size, batch_size=batch_size

)
# Rescale images (option 1)
train_ds = train_ds.map(rescale,
↪ num_parallel_calls=AUTOTUNE)
val_ds = val_ds.map(rescale,
↪ num_parallel_calls=AUTOTUNE)
# Configure the dataset for performance #
↪ https://www.tensorflow.org/tutorials/ima³⁵
train_ds =
↪ train_ds.cache().shuffle(1000).prefetch(
val_ds =
↪ val_ds.cache().prefetch(buffer_size=AUTO
# Define the model architecture
model = Sequential([

  # Rescaling(1. / 255,
  ↪ input_shape=(img_size[0],
  ↪ img_size[1], 3)), # Rescale images
  ↪ (option 2)
  # ADD CODE HERE
```

```
Conv2D(filters=32, kernel_size=(3, 3),
↪ activation='relu',
↪ input_shape=(img_size[0],
↪ img_size[1], 3)),
MaxPooling2D(pool_size=(2, 2)),
Conv2D(filters=64, kernel_size=(3, 3),
↪ activation='relu'),
MaxPooling2D(pool_size=(2, 2)), Flatten(),
Dense(units=64,          activation='relu'),          Dense(1,
activation='sigmoid')

])
# Compile the model # ADD CODE HERE
model.compile(optimizer='adam',
↪ loss='binary_crossentropy',
↪ metrics=['accuracy'])
# Define the early stopping callback for
↪ val_accuracy
# ADD CODE HERE
early_stop =
↪ EarlyStopping(monitor='val_accuracy',
↪ patience=5, verbose=1, min_delta=0.01)
```

```
# Show the model architecture (optional)
summarize_model(model)
# Train the model with early stopping
↪ callback
# ADD CODE HERE
model.fit(x=train_ds, epochs=5,
↪ validation_data=val_ds,
↪ callbacks=[early_stop])
return model
```

5 Natural language processing

5.1 Question

```
# Copyright (c) 2023, Troy Phat Tran (Mr.
    ↪ Troy).
    # Question:
    # Build and train a binary classifier for the
    ↪ language classification dataset. The
    ↪ dataset is typically a JSON array
```

```
# of 500 JSON objects. Each object has 3 keys:
↪ sentence, language_code, and is_english.
# We want our model to be able to determine
↪ whether a piece of text is "English or
↪ not".
# Your task is to fill in the missing parts of
↪ the code block (where commented as "ADD
↪ CODE HERE").
# Note: the dataset is imbalanced as there are
↪ more non-English sentences than English
↪ ones. To keep things simple,
# you don't need to handle data imbalance in
↪ this coding challenge.
import json import os
from urllib.request import urlretrieve
import numpy as np
from keras import Sequential
from        keras.src.models        import        load_model        from
keras.src.preprocessing.text import
↪ Tokenizer
from keras.src.utils import pad_sequences
```

```
def nlp_binary_model():
# Download the dataset
json_file        =        'language-classification.json'        if        not
os.path.exists(json_file):

    url =
    ↪ 'https://trientran.github.io/tf-prac
    urlretrieve(url=url,
    ↪ filename=json_file)

# Parse the JSON file
with open(file=json_file, mode='r',

    ↪ encoding='utf-8') as f: datastore = json.load(f)

# Extract texts and labels from JSON data
texts = [] labels = []

    for item in datastore: texts.append(item['sentence']) #
    ↪ replace with the
    ↪ sentence/paragraph/text field in
    ↪ the real test JSON file
```

```python
    labels.append(item['is_english']) #
    ↪ replace with the label field in the
    ↪ real test JSON file

    # Predefined constants
    max_length = 25
    trunc_type = 'pre' # Can be replaced with
    ↪ 'post'
    vocab_size = 500
    padding_type = 'pre' # Can be replaced
    ↪ with 'post'
    embedding_dim = 32 oov_tok = "<OOV>" training_size = 400
    # Split the dataset into training and
    ↪ validation sets

    training_sentences = texts[0:training_size] testing_sentences =
texts[training_size:]     training_labels     =     labels[0:training_size]
validation_labels = labels[training_size:]
    # Tokenize the texts
    tokenizer = Tokenizer(num_words=vocab_size,
    ↪ oov_token=oov_tok)
    tokenizer.fit_on_texts(training_sentences)
```

```
training_sequences =
↪ tokenizer.texts_to_sequences(training_se
testing_sequences =
↪ tokenizer.texts_to_sequences(testing_sen
# Pad the sequences
padded_training_set =
↪ pad_sequences(sequences=training_sequenc

                                          ↪ maxl
                                          ↪ padd


   ↪ trun

padded_validation_set =
↪ pad_sequences(sequences=testing_sequence




                                          ↪ ma




                                          ↪ pa




                                          ↪ tr
# Convert the labels to numpy array
   training_labels = np.array(training_labels)
```

```python
validation_labels =
↪ np.array(validation_labels)
# Define the model architecture
model = Sequential([

    # ADD CODE HERE

])
# Compile the model # ADD CODE HERE
# Define an early stopping callback
↪ (optional)
# ADD CODE HERE
# Train the model # ADD CODE HERE
return model


# ================DO NOT EDIT THIS
↪ PART================================
if name == ' main ':
# Run and save your model
my_model = nlp_binary_model()
```

```
filepath = "nlp_binary_model.h5" my_model.save(filepath)
# Reload the saved model
saved_model = load_model(filepath)
# Show the model architecture
saved_model.summary()
```

5.2 Solution

```
import json import os
    from urllib.request import urlretrieve
    import numpy as np
    from keras import Sequential
    from keras.layers import Embedding, Dense from keras.src.callbacks
import EarlyStopping from keras.src.layers import
    ↪ GlobalAveragePooling1D
    from keras.src.models import load_model
```

```python
from keras.src.preprocessing.text import
↪ Tokenizer
from keras.src.utils import pad_sequences


def nlp_binary_model():
    # Download the dataset
    json_file        =        'language-classification.json'        if        not
os.path.exists(json_file):

    url =
    ↪ 'https://trientran.github.io/tf-prac
    urlretrieve(url=url,
    ↪ filename=json_file)

    # Parse the JSON file
    with open(file=json_file, mode='r',

    ↪ encoding='utf-8') as f: datastore = json.load(f)

    # Extract texts and labels from JSON data
    texts = [] labels = []
    for item in datastore:
```

```python
    texts.append(item['sentence']) #
↪ replace with the
↪ sentence/paragraph/text field in
↪ the real test JSON file
    labels.append(item['is_english']) #
↪ replace with the label field in the
↪ real test JSON file

# Predefined constants
max_length = 25
trunc_type = 'pre' # Can be replaced with
↪ 'post'
vocab_size = 500
padding_type = 'pre' # Can be replaced
↪ with 'post'
embedding_dim = 32 oov_tok = "<OOV>" training_size = 400
# Split the dataset into training and
↪ validation sets
training_sentences = texts[0:training_size] testing_sentences =
texts[training_size:]    training_labels    =    labels[0:training_size]
validation_labels = labels[training_size:]
```

```python
# Tokenize the texts
tokenizer = Tokenizer(num_words=vocab_size,
↪ oov_token=oov_tok)
tokenizer.fit_on_texts(training_sentences) training_sequences =
↪ tokenizer.texts_to_sequences(training_se
testing_sequences =
↪ tokenizer.texts_to_sequences(testing_sen
# Pad the sequences
padded_training_set =
↪ pad_sequences(sequences=training_sequenc

                                        ↪ maxl
                                        ↪ padd


    ↪ trun

padded_validation_set =
↪ pad_sequences(sequences=testing_sequence




                                        ↪ ma




                                        ↪ pa




                                        ↪ tr
```

```python
# Convert the labels to numpy array training_labels =
np.array(training_labels) validation_labels =
    ↪ np.array(validation_labels)
    # Define the model architecture
    model = Sequential([

    # ADD CODE HERE
    Embedding(input_dim=vocab_size,
    ↪ output_dim=embedding_dim,
    ↪ input_length=max_length),
    GlobalAveragePooling1D(),                        Dense(units=1,
    activation='sigmoid')

])
# Compile the model # ADD CODE HERE
model.compile(loss='binary_crossentropy',
↪ optimizer='adam', metrics=['accuracy'])
# Define an early stopping callback # ADD CODE HERE
early_stop =
↪ EarlyStopping(monitor='val_loss',
↪ patience=5)
```

```
# Train the model # ADD CODE HERE
model.fit(x=padded_training_set,

  y=training_labels, epochs=50,

  ↪ validation_data=(padded_valida
  ↪ validation_labels),

callbacks=[early_stop]) return model
```

6 Time series and sequences

6.1 Question

```
# Copyright (c) 2023, Troy Phat Tran (Mr.
  ↪ Troy).
# Question:
```

```
# Build and train a Sequential model that can
↪ predict the level of humidity for 5 cities
↪ over the time using the
# cities-humidity.csv dataset. The normalized
↪ dataset should have a mean absolute error
↪ (MAE) of 0.15 or less.
# Your task is to fill in the missing parts of
↪ the code block (where commented as "ADD
↪ CODE HERE").
# Specific requirements:
# 1. Input shape: (batch_size = 8, n_past = 6,
↪ n_features = 5)
# n_past means a window of the past 6
↪ observations
# n_features means 5 features (cities) to
↪ predict
# 2. Output shape: (batch_size = 8, n_future =
↪ 6, n_features = 5)
# n_future means the next 6 observations to
↪ predict
```

```python
import os
from urllib.request import urlretrieve
import pandas as pd
from keras import Sequential
from keras.callbacks import Callback from
keras.src.saving.saving_api import
↪ load_model
from tensorflow.python.data import Dataset from
tensorflow.python.framework.random_seed
↪ import set_seed


def time_series_model():
    # Download the dataset
    csv_file = 'cities-humidity.csv' if not os.path.exists(csv_file):

        url =
        ↪ 'https://trientran.github.io/tf-prac
        urlretrieve(url=url, filename=csv_file)

    # Read the CSV
    df = pd.read_csv(csv_file, sep=",",
    ↪ index_col='date', header=0)
    # Normalize the data
```

```
data = df.values
data = data - data.min(axis=0) data = data / data.max(axis=0)
# Define a variable to hold the number of
↪ features/cities in the dataset.
n_features = len(df.columns)
# Some default constants (feel free to
↪ update these if the real exam provides
↪ different ones)
n_past = 6
n_future = 6
batch_size = 8
# Set seed to persist training results
set_seed(1)
# Split into training and validation sets.
split_time = int(len(data) * 0.5) x_train = data[:split_time] x_valid
= data[split_time:]
# Create windowed train and validation sets
```

```python
train_set =
↪ windowed_dataset(series=x_train,
↪ batch_size=batch_size, n_past=n_past,
↪ n_future=n_future)
valid_set =
↪ windowed_dataset(series=x_valid,
↪ batch_size=batch_size, n_past=n_past,
↪ n_future=n_future)
# Define your model
model = Sequential([

  # ADD CODE HERE

])
# Compile the model # ADD CODE HERE
# Optional: Print out summary log to
↪ double-check input and output shapes
# ADD CODE HERE (optional)
# Optional: Define callbacks # ADD CODE HERE (optional)
# Trains the model # ADD CODE HERE
```

```
return model


class MyCallback(Callback):

    def on_epoch_end(self, epoch, logs=None): if logs is None:
    logs = {}
    val_mae = logs.get('val_mae') if val_mae <= 0.15: # Very
    ↪ importantly, you must change this
    ↪ number if the test expects a
    ↪ certain limit of MAE.
    # For example, this test requires
    ↪ an MAE of 0.15 or less. So it
    ↪ makes sense to set this number
    ↪ to 0.15
    print(f"\nReached {val_mae} Mean
    ↪ Absolute Error after {epoch}
    ↪ epochs so stopping training!")
    self.model.stop_training = True



# A function to create windowed dataset.
    ↪ Derived from
```

```
# ↪ https://colab.research.google.com/github/lmo
    def windowed_dataset(series, batch_size,
    ↪ n_past, n_future):
    ds          =          Dataset.from_tensor_slices(series)          ds          =
ds.window(size=n_past + n_future,
    ↪ shift=1, drop_remainder=True)
    ds = ds.flat_map(lambda w: w.batch(n_past +
    ↪ n_future))
    ds = ds.map(lambda w: (w[:n_past],
    ↪ w[n_past:]))
    return ds.batch(batch_size).prefetch(1)


# ===============DO NOT EDIT THE
    ↪ BELOW===============================
    # Train and save the model
    if name == ' main ':
    # Run and save your model my_model = time_series_model()
filepath = "time_series_model.h5" my_model.save(filepath)
    # Reload the saved model
    saved_model = load_model(filepath)
```

```python
# Show the model architecture
saved_model.summary()
```

6.2 Solution

```python
import os
    from urllib.request import urlretrieve
    import pandas as pd
    from keras import Sequential
    from keras.callbacks import EarlyStopping,
    ↪ Callback
    from keras.src.layers import Bidirectional,
    ↪ LSTM, Dense, Reshape
    from keras.src.saving.saving_api import
    ↪ load_model
    from         tensorflow.python.data      import      Dataset      from
tensorflow.python.framework.random_seed
    ↪ import set_seed


def time_series_model():
```

```python
# Download the dataset
csv_file = 'cities-humidity.csv' if not os.path.exists(csv_file):

    url =
    ↪ 'https://trientran.github.io/tf-prac
    urlretrieve(url=url, filename=csv_file)

# Read the CSV
df = pd.read_csv(csv_file, sep=",",
↪ index_col='date', header=0)
# Normalize the data
data = df.values
data = data - data.min(axis=0) data = data / data.max(axis=0)
# Define a variable to hold the number of
↪ features/cities in the dataset.
n_features = len(df.columns)
# Some default constants (feel free to
↪ update these if the real exam provides
↪ different ones)
n_past = 6
n_future = 6
batch_size = 8
```

```
# Set seed to persist training results
set_seed(1)
# Split into training and validation sets.
split_time = int(len(data) * 0.5) x_train = data[:split_time] x_valid
= data[split_time:]
# Create windowed train and validation sets
train_set =
↪ windowed_dataset(series=x_train,
↪ batch_size=batch_size, n_past=n_past,
↪ n_future=n_future)
valid_set =
↪ windowed_dataset(series=x_valid,
↪ batch_size=batch_size, n_past=n_past,
↪ n_future=n_future)
# Define your model
model = Sequential([

    # ADD CODE HERE
    Bidirectional(LSTM(32,
    ↪ return_sequences=True,
    ↪ input_shape=(n_past, n_features))),
    Bidirectional(LSTM(32)),
```

```python
    Dense(n_features * n_future,
    ↪ activation='relu'),
    Reshape((n_future, n_features)),

])
# Compile the model # ADD CODE HERE
model.compile(loss='mse', optimizer='adam',
↪ metrics=['mae'])
# Build the model and print out summary log
↪ to double-check input and output shapes
# ADD CODE HERE
model.build(input_shape=(batch_size,
↪ n_past, n_features))
model.summary()
input_shape = model.layers[0].input_shape print(f'Input shape:
{input_shape}')
    # Define callbacks # ADD CODE HERE
early_stopping_1 =
↪ EarlyStopping(monitor='val_mae',
↪ mode='min', patience=10, verbose=1,
↪ min_delta=0.005) # optional
early_stopping_2 = MyCallback()
```

```python
# Trains the model # ADD CODE HERE
model.fit(train_set, epochs=1000,
↪ validation_data=valid_set,
↪ callbacks=[early_stopping_2])
# model.fit(train_set, epochs=1000,
↪ validation_data=valid_set,
↪ callbacks=[early_stopping_1,
↪ early_stopping_2])
return model


class MyCallback(Callback):

    def on_epoch_end(self, epoch, logs=None): if logs is None:
    logs = {}
    val_mae = logs.get('val_mae') if val_mae <= 0.15: # Very
    ↪ importantly, you must change this
    ↪ number if the test expects a
    ↪ certain limit of MAE.
```

```
    # For example, this test requires
    ↪ an MAE of 0.15 or less. So it
    ↪ makes sense to set this number
    ↪ to 0.15
    print(f"\nReached {val_mae} Mean
    ↪ Absolute Error after {epoch}
    ↪ epochs so stopping training!")
    self.model.stop_training = True


# A function to create windowed dataset.
    ↪ Derived from #
    ↪ https://colab.research.google.com/github/lmo
def windowed_dataset(series, batch_size,
    ↪ n_past, n_future):
    ds        =         Dataset.from_tensor_slices(series)        ds        =
ds.window(size=n_past + n_future,
    ↪ shift=1, drop_remainder=True)
    ds = ds.flat_map(lambda w: w.batch(n_past +
    ↪ n_future))
    ds = ds.map(lambda w: (w[:n_past],
    ↪ w[n_past:]))
    return ds.batch(batch_size).prefetch(1)
```

7 Exam procedure

7.1 Step by step

Review the candidate handbook

_You are encouraged to read the candidate handbook (https://www.tensorflow.org/static/extras/cert/TF[36] and the setting-up-TF PDF (https://www.tensorflow.org/extras/cert/Setting Up[37] before taking the exam. Even though this course covers almost everything about the exam, there may be additional information worth noting in the handbook.

Register for the exam

Head to https://app.trueability.com/google-[38] certificates/ tensorflow-developer[39] and hit PUR- CHASE THE EXAM.

____Read the instructions from trueabil- ity for instructions for taking the exam: https://utility.trueability.com/google/tensor-[40] flow/ Instructions for taking the TensorFlow Certific[41]

---

36. https://www.tensorflow.org/static/extras/cert/TF_Certificate_Candidate_Handbook.pdf

37. https://www.tensorflow.org/extras/cert/Setting_Up_TF_Developer_Certificate_Exam.pdf

38. https://app.trueability.com/google-certificates/tensorflow-developer

39. https://app.trueability.com/google-certificates/tensorflow-developer

40.　　　https://utility.trueability.com/google/tensor-flow/
Instructions_for_taking_the_TensorFlow_Certificate_exam.pdf

41.　　　https://utility.trueability.com/google/tensor-flow/
Instructions_for_taking_the_TensorFlow_Certificate_exam.pdf

Log in with a Gmail Account, then upload your picture ID (your driver's license or passport), and provide payment information.

Prepare your exam environment

Please refer to the section "Prepare your exam en- vironment" for how to fully set up your computer and get ready for the exam.

Take and submit the exam

You can log in and sit for the exam anytime within six months of purchasing it. The exam must be completed within five hours at maximum.

Receive your TensorFlow Certificate

After submitting your exam, you should receive the result within 24 hours via email or you can check the result status at https://trueability.com[42].

7.2 Summary of Useful Tips

Tips for taking the TensorFlow Developer Certificate Exam:

Software and Package Management:

• Install the correct versions of Python pack- ages, as required in page 10 of the handbook https://www.tensorflow.org/extras/cert/Settin[43] This is usually done automatically using re- quirements.txt

---

42. https://trueability.com/

43. https://www.tensorflow.org/extras/cert/Setting_Up_TF_Developer_Certificate_Exam.pdf

• If you encounter difficulties automatically installing packages, just try again or try installing them manually via the Python Packages panel or the settings menu (set- tings/Project:[project name])/Python Inter- preter).

• If the TensorFlow package installation fails on the first attempt, try again.

• The latest version of PyCharm may not be com- patible with TensorFlow Developer Certificate plugin. If that's the case, download an older version of Pycharm.

Specific Software Issues and Solutions:

____• On Microsoft Windows, when run- ning a Python solution file, if you encounter "ImportError: cannot im- port name ' no nep50 warning' from 'numpy.core. ufunc config'", resolve it by uninstalling the current numpy version and installing version 1.23.0.

_• When working with JSON files, declare utf-8 encoding to avoid UnicodeDecodeErrors. Use: with open(json file, 'r', encoding='utf-8') as f.

—• For Mac users, if you receive an URLEr- ror related to SSL certificate verification (url- lib.error.URLError: ¡urlopen error [SSL: CER- TIFICATE VERIFY FAILED]), install an SSL

certificate by navigating to Finder ¿ Appli- cations ¿ Python3.8 folder (or your Python version) and running the "Install Certifi- cates.command" file.

Model Output Focus:

• The exam primarily evaluates the output of your model. Ensure the first and last layers of the Sequential model are correctly defined.

• Pay attention to the input shape, which must match the required one.

Efficiency in Model Training:

• For image classification problems, consider setting the number of epochs between 10-

20 and early callback patience to 3-5. This approach helps identify ineffective models quickly, allowing for timely fine-tuning and re-training.

• If you have slow internet and need to retrain an image classification model, consider com- menting out or conditionally controlling the dataset downloading section to prevent redun- dant downloads, saving valuable time.

• If your computer is not powerful, start with RGB Image classification, as it may take longer to train. Work on other tasks during this time.

• Alternatively, use Google Colab or Kaggle note- books with premium processors for training, and then download the h5 model to your Py- Charm project.

These tips are structured to provide a clearer under- standing and easier recall during the exam.

7.3 Share your achievement with the world

After you have passed the exam, you should be re- ceiving a congratulation email from TrueAbility with some instruction on how to share your achievement with the world. There are 2 options for you:

First, Certificate Net- work (attach screenshot from https://developers.google.com/certification/directo[44]

---

44.   https://developers.google.com/certification/directory/tensorflow

"You are now eligible to be listed among fellow Ten- sorFlow developers in the TensorFlow Certificate Net- work. This network is a great place for recruiters to find potential talent and for you to see your peers who have also achieved this accomplishment. If you are in- terested in joining this network, just fill out the Google form, and you will be added to our directory within 2 weeks of your submission."

The second option is, to add a Digital Certificate & Badge to your LinkedIn or Github profile:

"You will be receiving an email from Accredible (support@credential.net) with your digital certificate and badge within the next two weeks. We encourage you to share this accomplishment on your resume and platforms like Github and LinkedIn to be recognized as a top candidate for recruiters seeking TensorFlow developers."

Here is my certificate badge on my LinkedIn pro- file (open https://www.linkedin.com/in/trientran/
).

And that concludes this book, please connect with me on Linkedin, I am looking forward to seeing your achievement and learning from you as well.

7.4 All resources

Resources used in this course:

• All the practice tests and solutions in Python format (*.py). They have the same format as the real exams and should be run using Pycharm IDE. We will go through them one by one later: https://drive.google.com/drive/folders/1tLiXS[45]

• All the practice tests and solutions in notebook format (*.ipynb). If you are fa- miliar with Jupyter/Google Colab/Kaggle notebooks. They are ready for you to run: https://drive.google.com/drive/folders/1201t[46] dVzKfW1xokqHstJfk9-l[47]

• Python ebook

• TensorFlow certificate homepage: https://www.tensorflow.org/certificate

• Candidate handbook:

• https://www.tensorflow.org/static/extras/cert[48]

• Handbook for setting up your computer for the exam: https://www.tensorflow.org/extras/cert/Settin[49]

---

45.   https://drive.google.com/drive/folders/1tLiXSeCkkAMohkEamForaQNFwi3xszA5

46.   https://drive.google.com/drive/folders/1201tNVcv27F-dVzKfW1xokqHstJfk9-l

47.   https://drive.google.com/drive/folders/1201tNVcv27F-dVzKfW1xokqHstJfk9-l

48.   https://www.tensorflow.org/static/extras/cert/TF_Certificate_Candidate_Handbook.pdf

49.   https://www.tensorflow.org/extras/cert/Setting_Up_TF_Developer_Certificate_Exam.pdf

- Trueability's handbook (Trueability is affiliated with Google's TensorFlow to conduct the exam)

  ____• https://utility.trueability.com/google/tensor-[50]   flow/ Instructions for taking the TensorFlow Ce[51]

- My certificate for your reference: https://www.credential.net/f7b087a1-a977-[52] 4b84-bdd6-fb7d92eae41b[53]

- Certificate network:

  https://developers.google.com/certification/di[54]

---

50. https://utility.trueability.com/google/tensor-flow/

    Instructions_for_taking_the_TensorFlow_Certificate_exam.pdf

51. https://utility.trueability.com/google/tensor-flow/

    Instructions_for_taking_the_TensorFlow_Certificate_exam.pdf

52. https://www.credential.net/f7b087a1-a977-4b84-bdd6-fb7d92eae41b

53. https://www.credential.net/f7b087a1-a977-4b84-bdd6-fb7d92eae41b

54. https://developers.google.com/certification/directory/tensorflow

Don't miss out!

Visit the website below and you can sign up to receive emails whenever Mr Troy publishes a new book. There's no charge and no obligation.

https://books2read.com/r/B-A-UAHDB-QZGVC

BOOKS 2 READ

Connecting independent readers to independent writers.